# Bible Verse
# Coloring Book For Adults

## 52 Inspiring Designs For Relaxation & Stress Relief

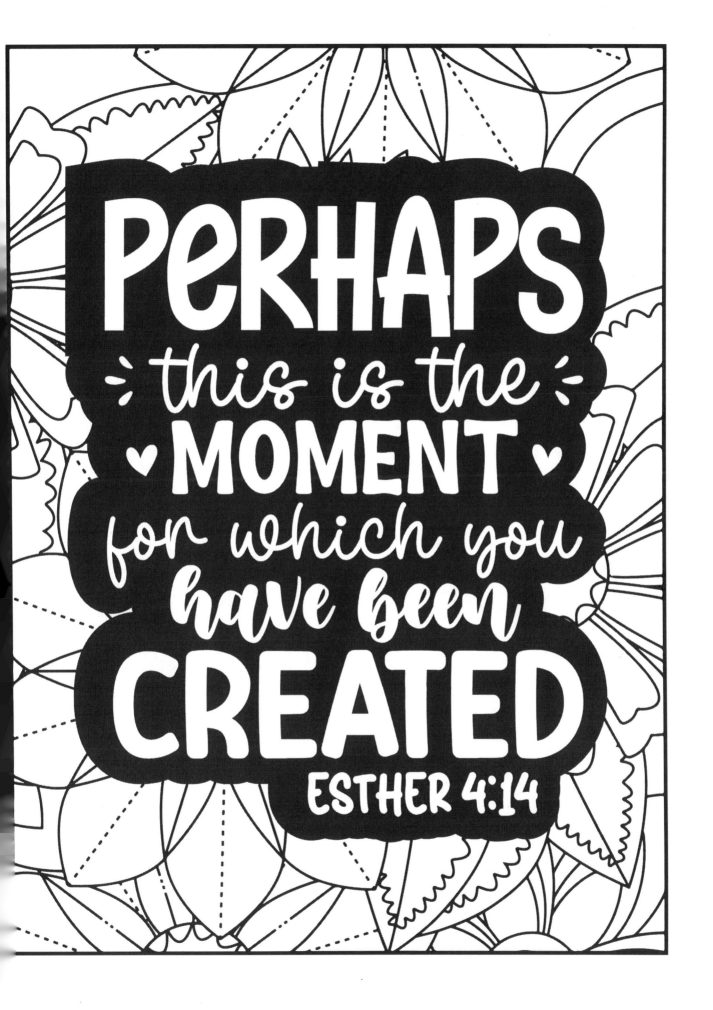

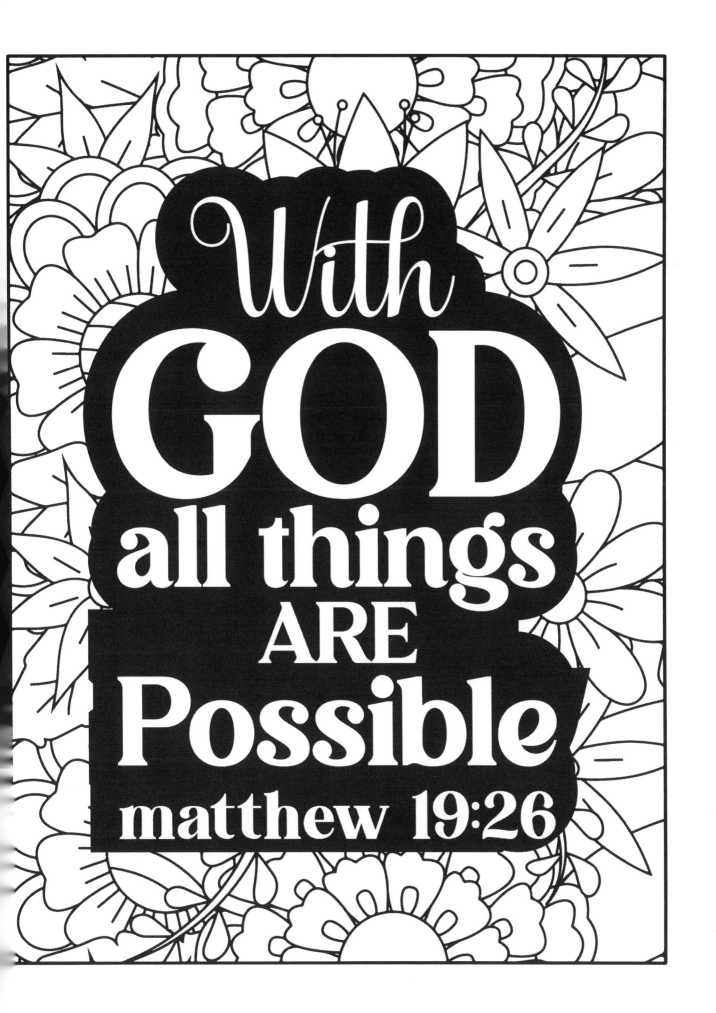

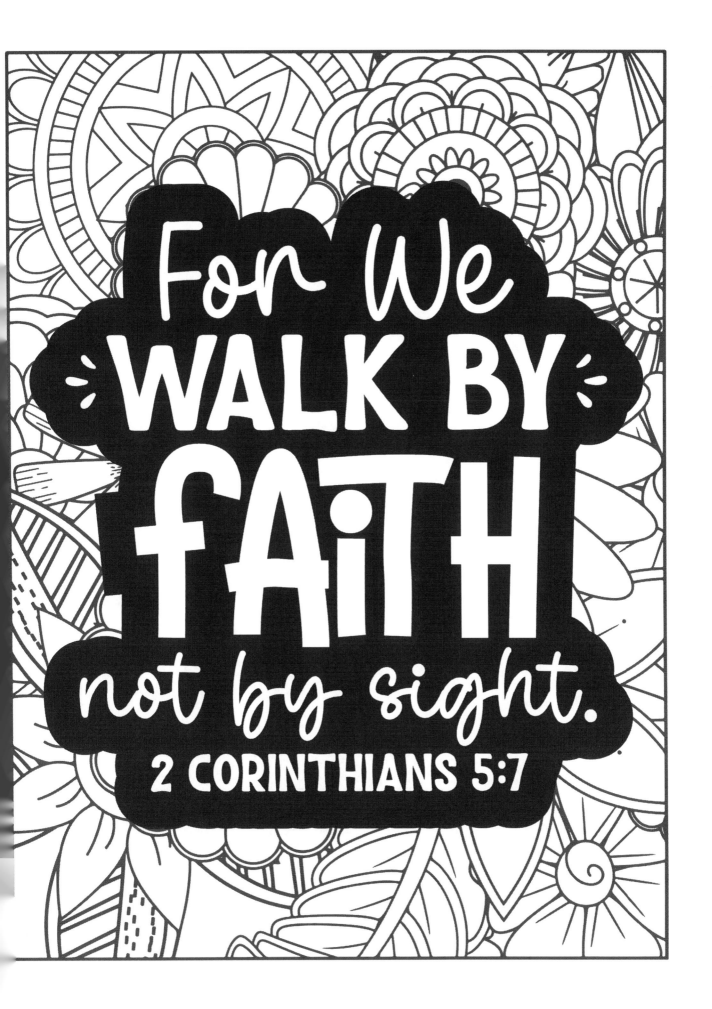

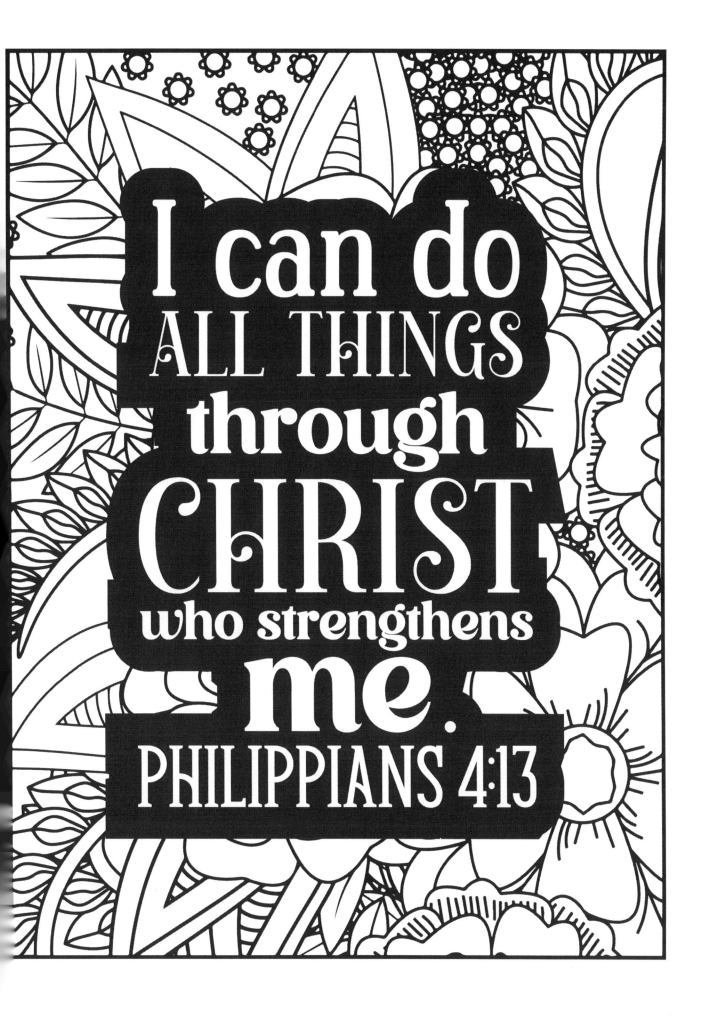

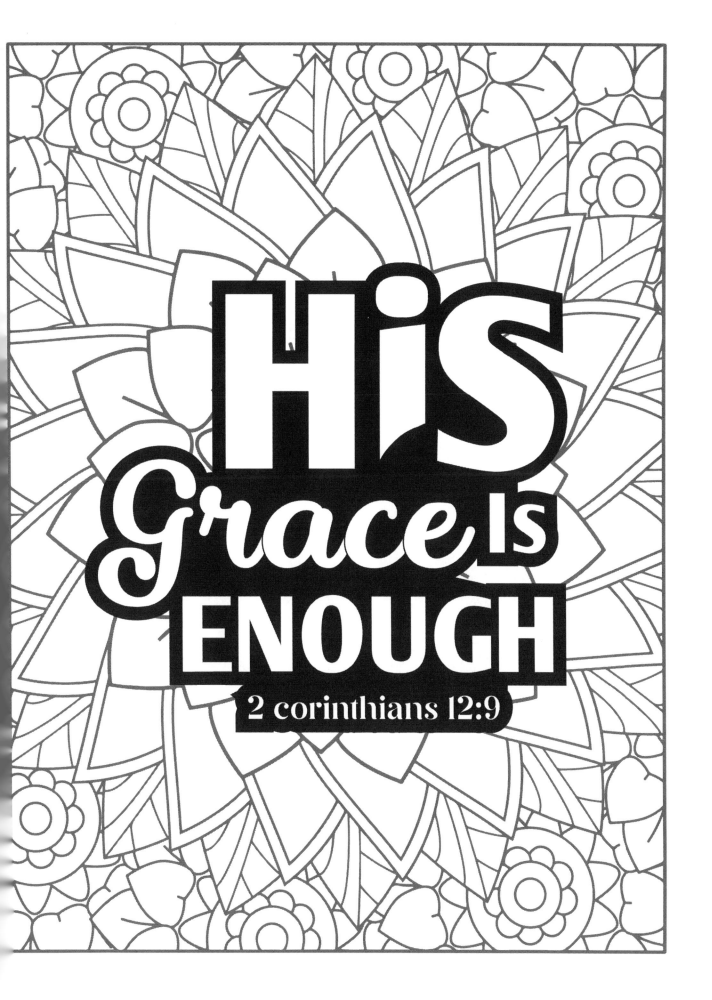

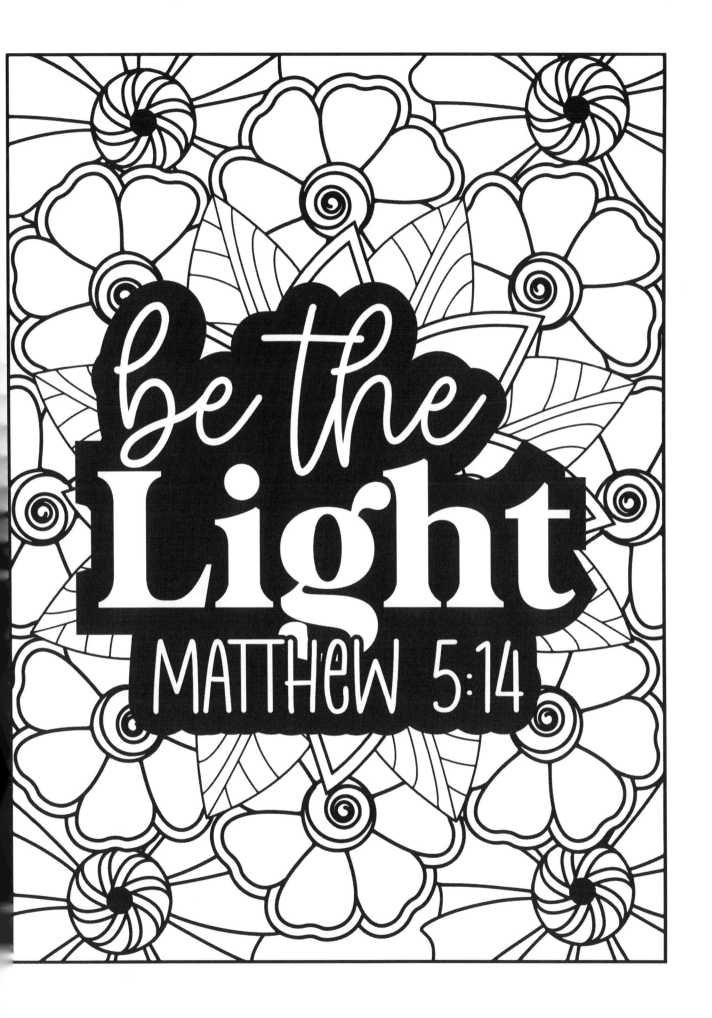

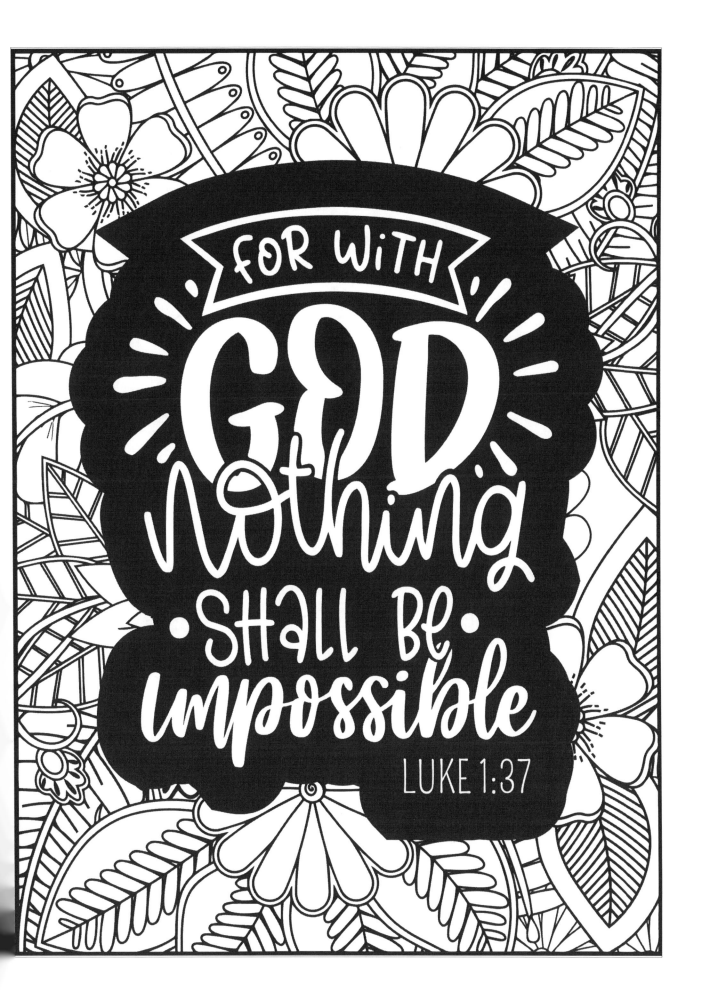

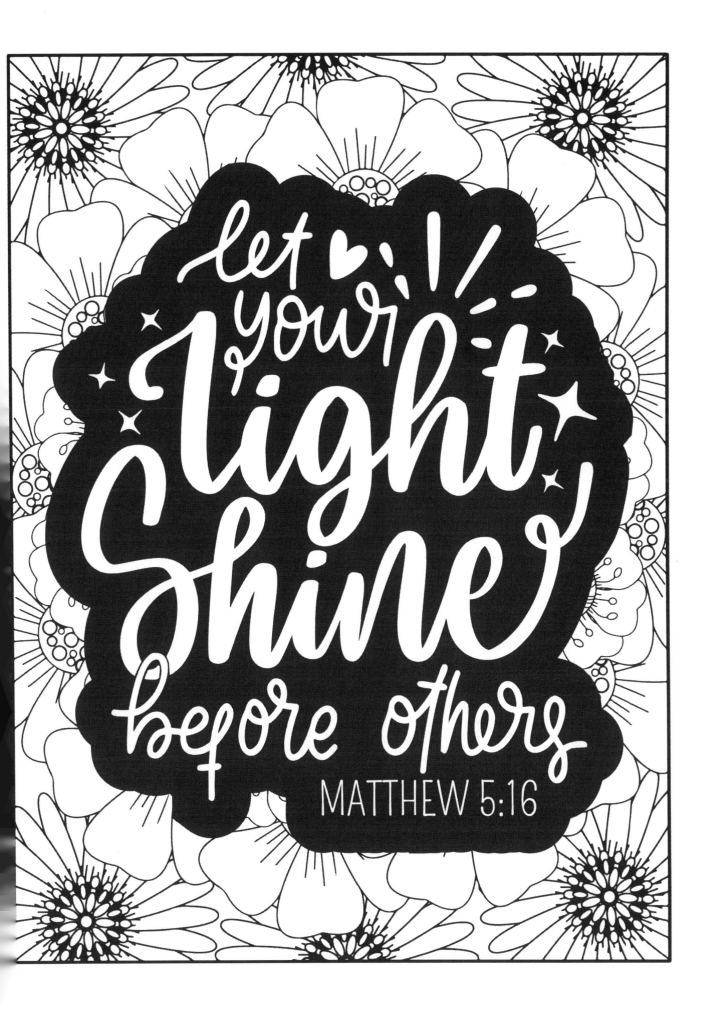

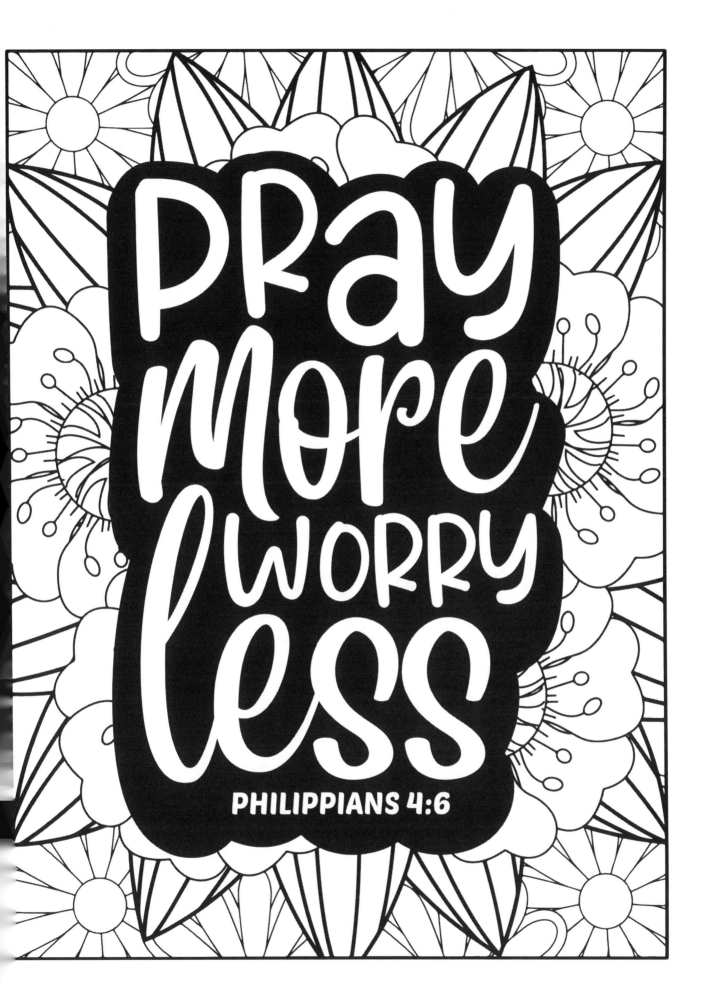

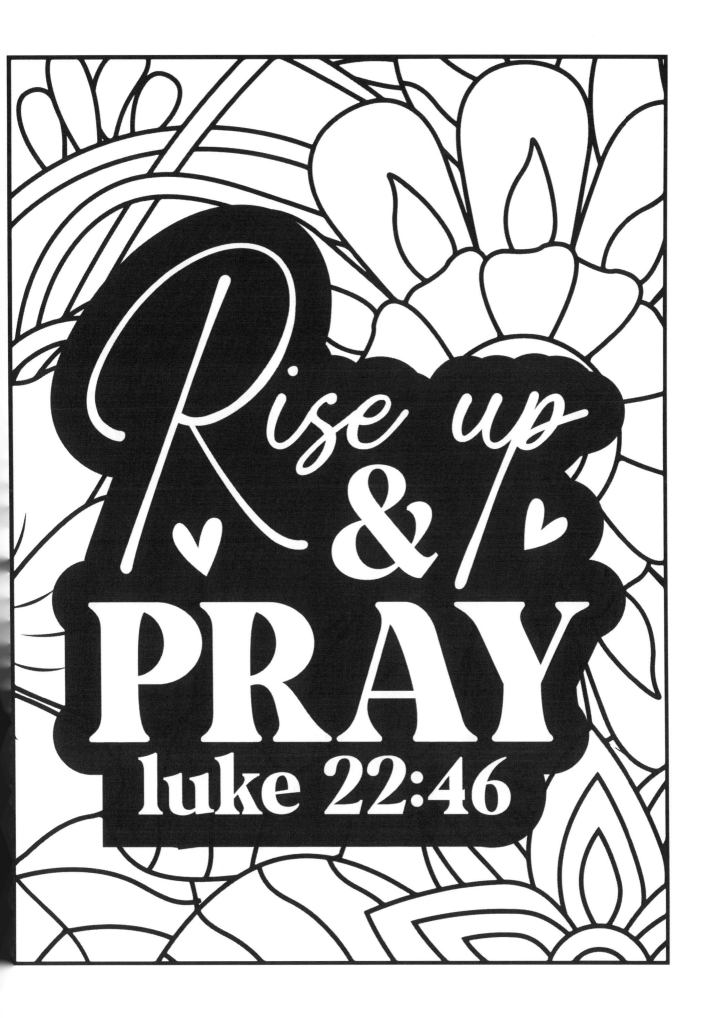

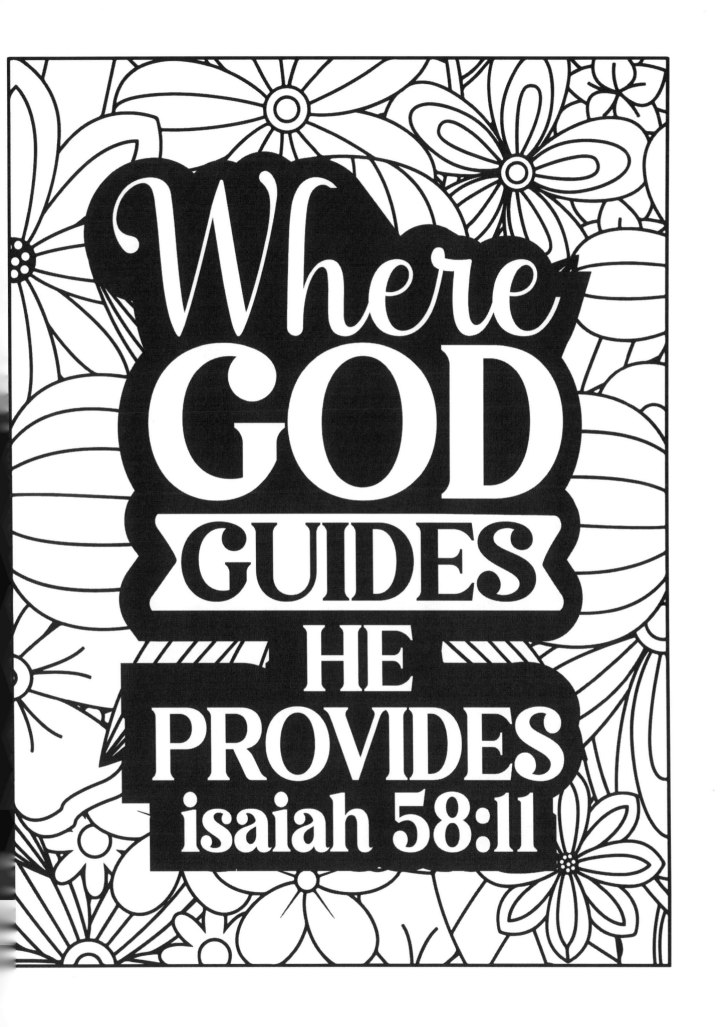

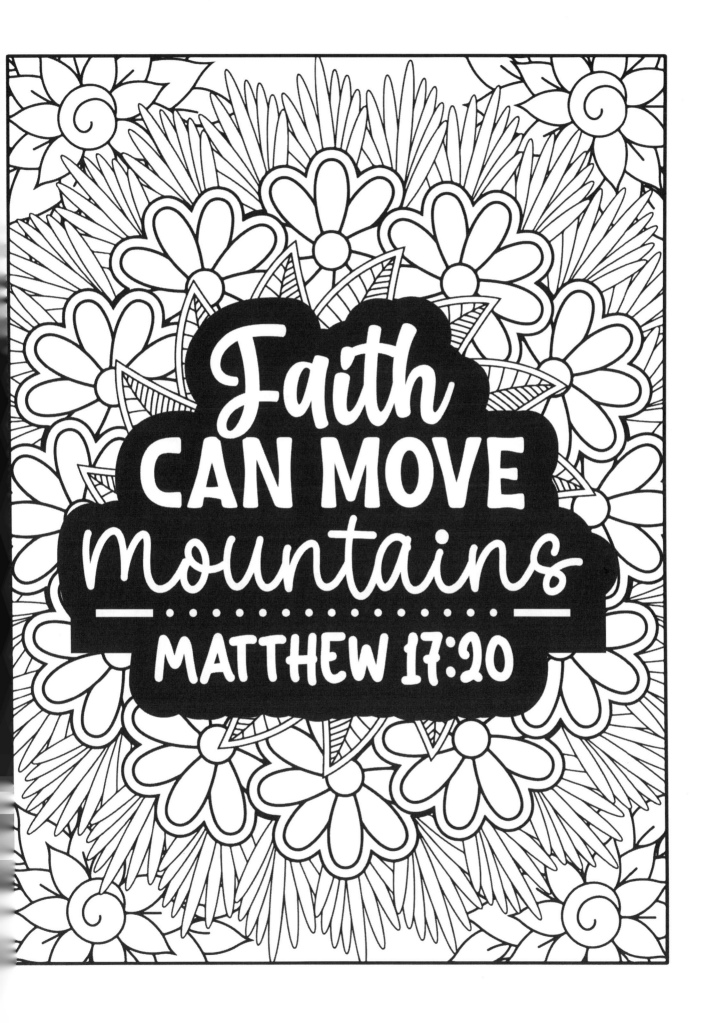

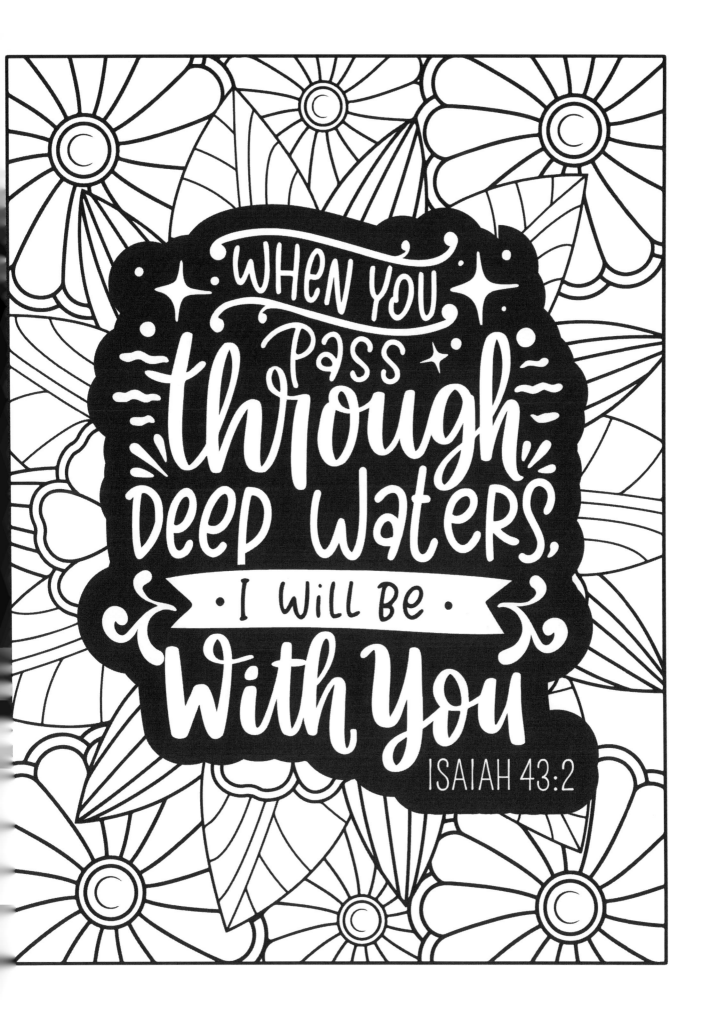

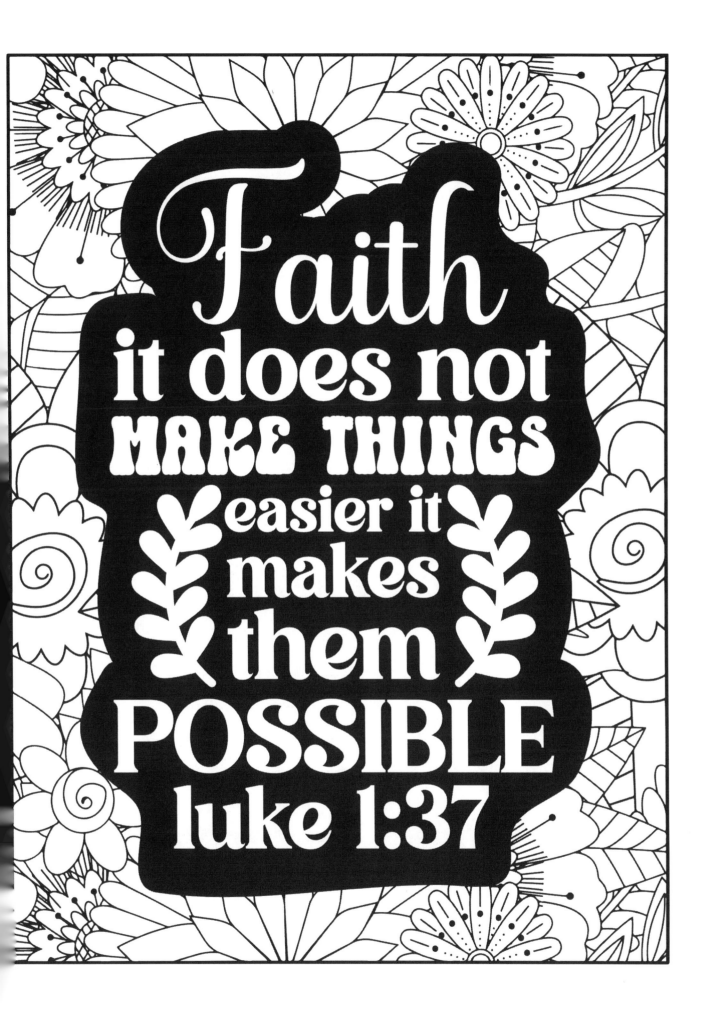

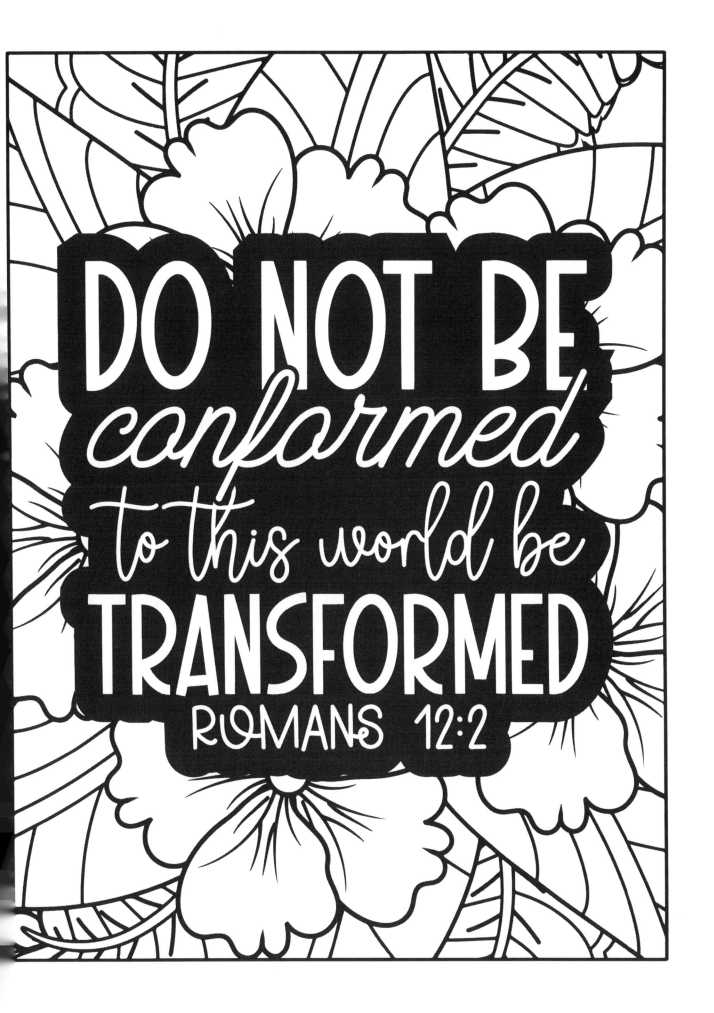

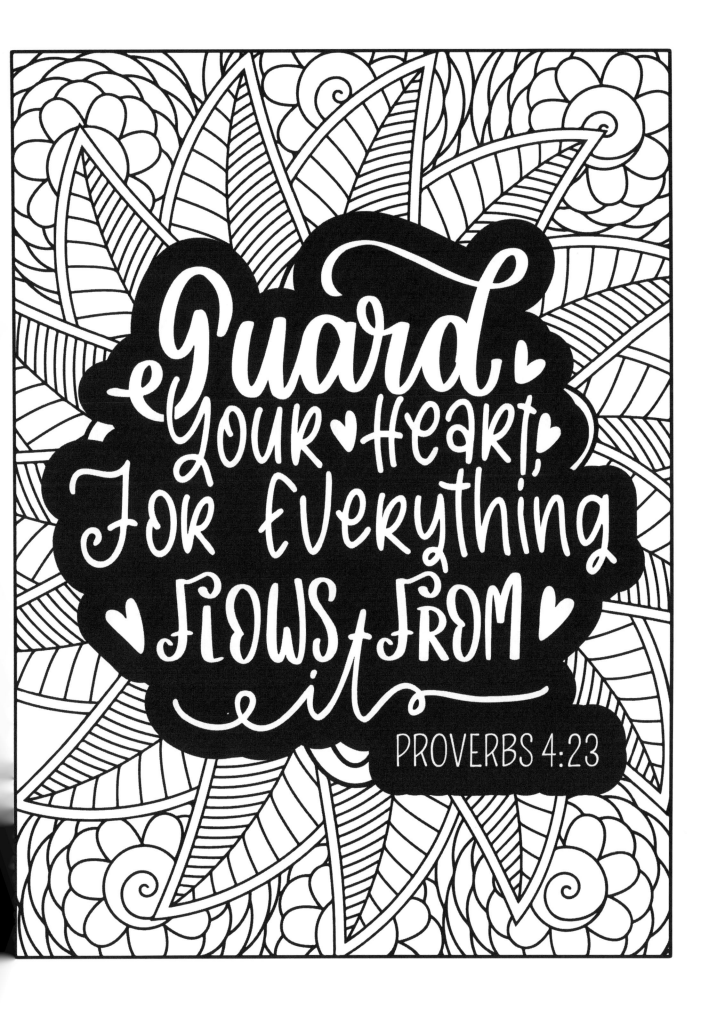

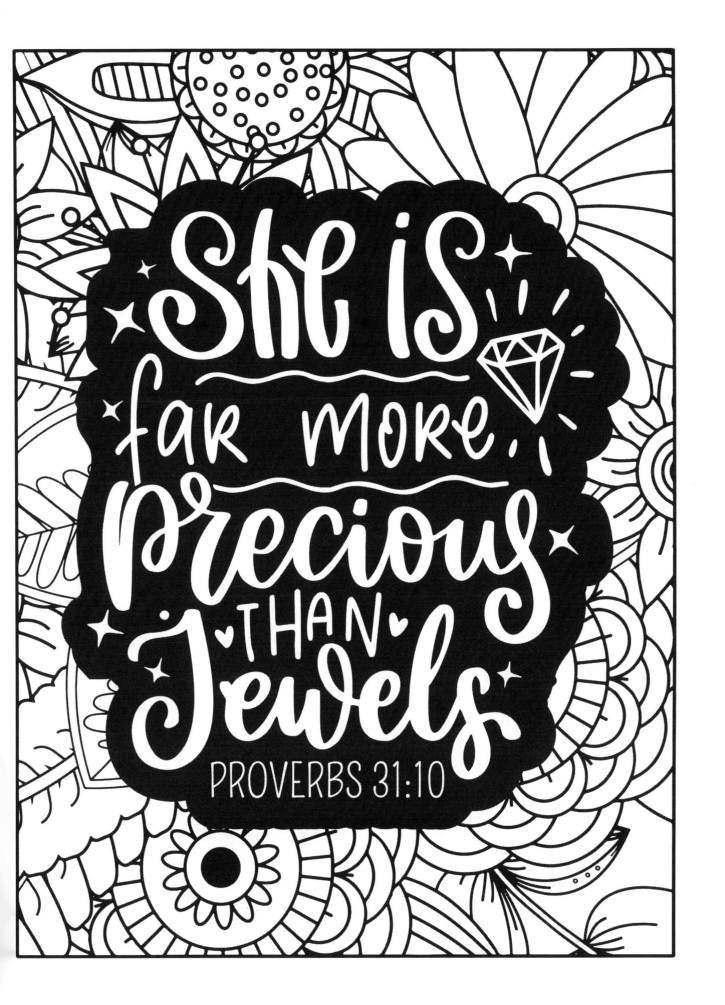

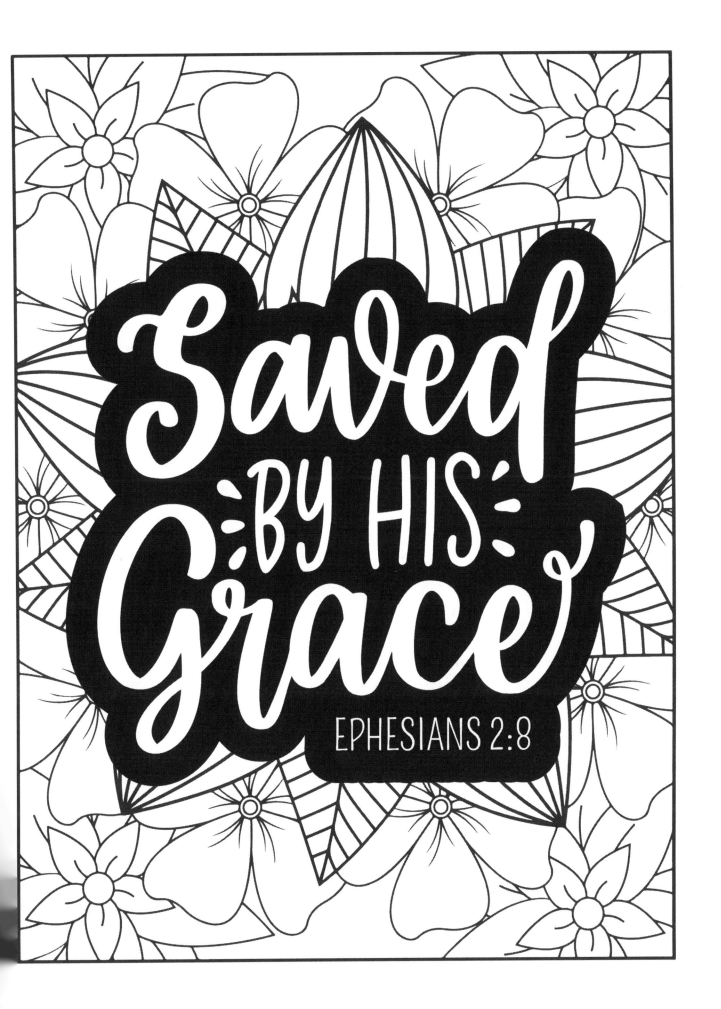

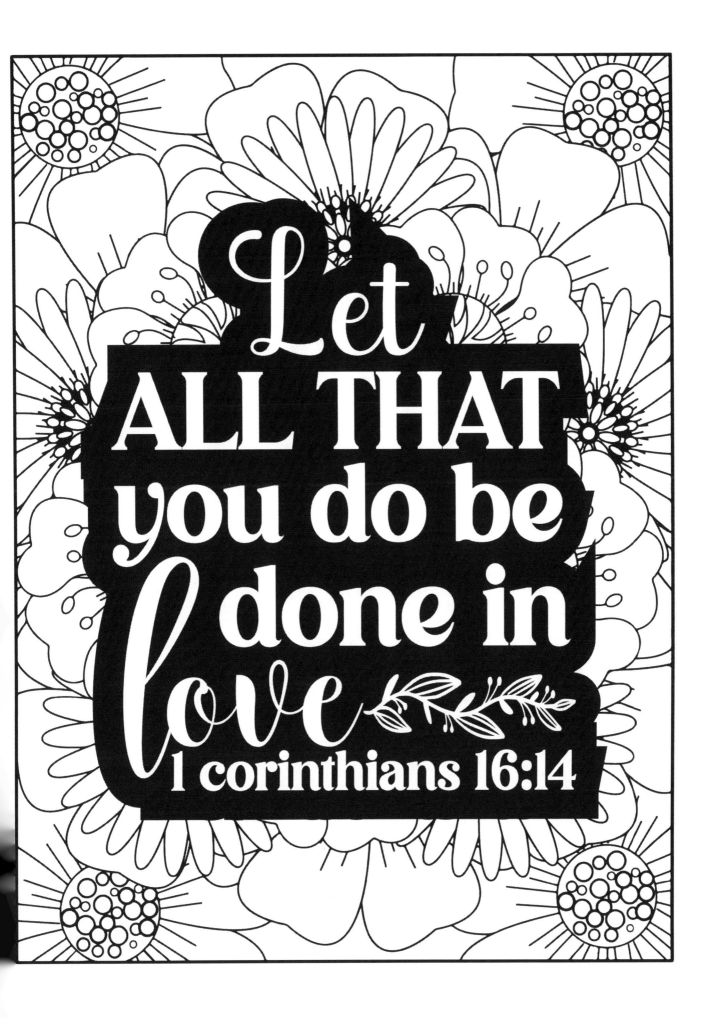

Let ALL THAT you do be done in love

1 corinthians 16:14

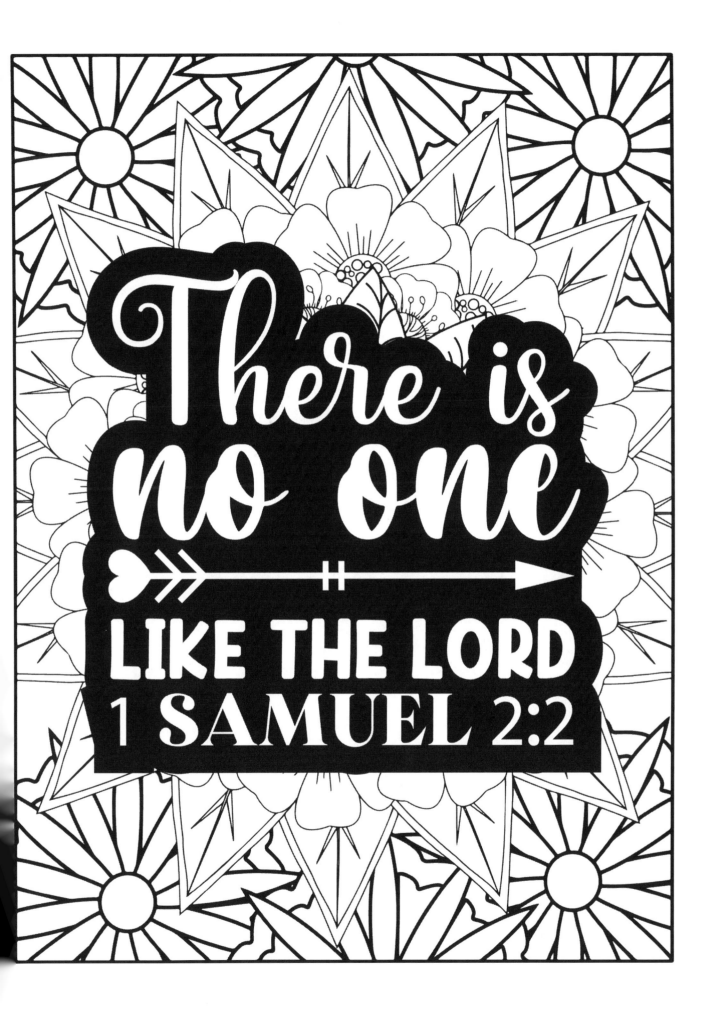

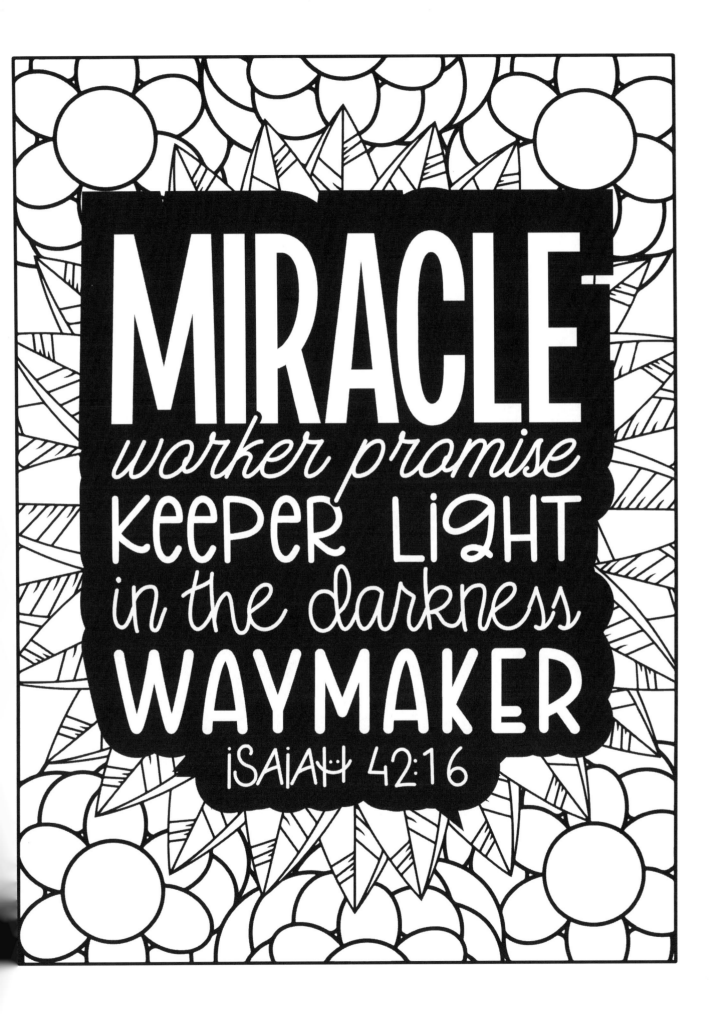

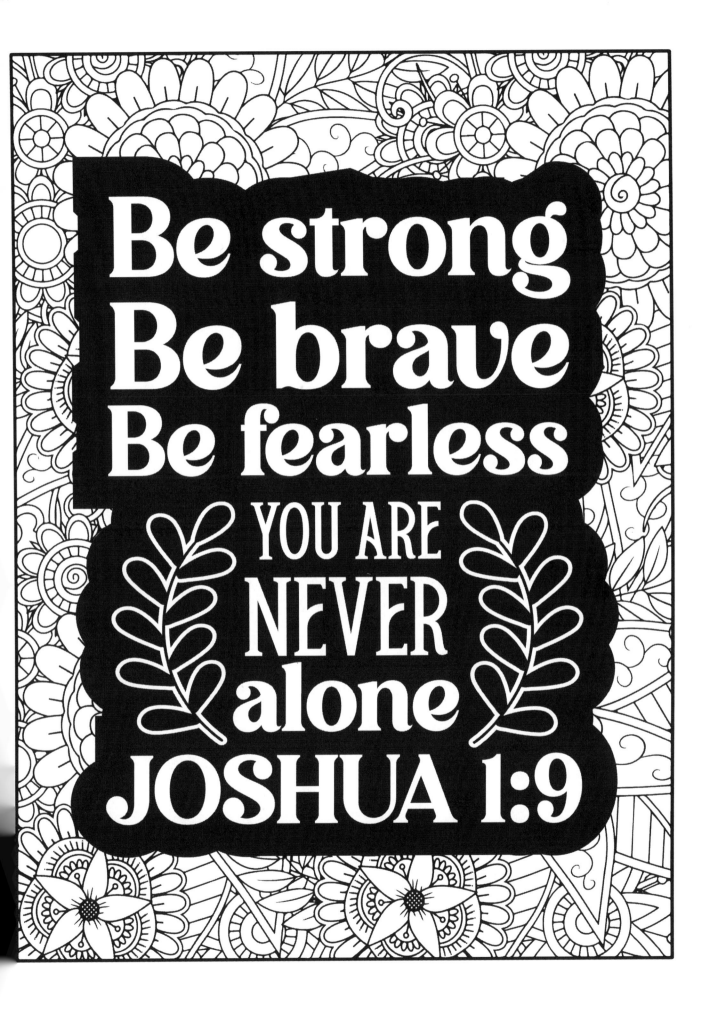

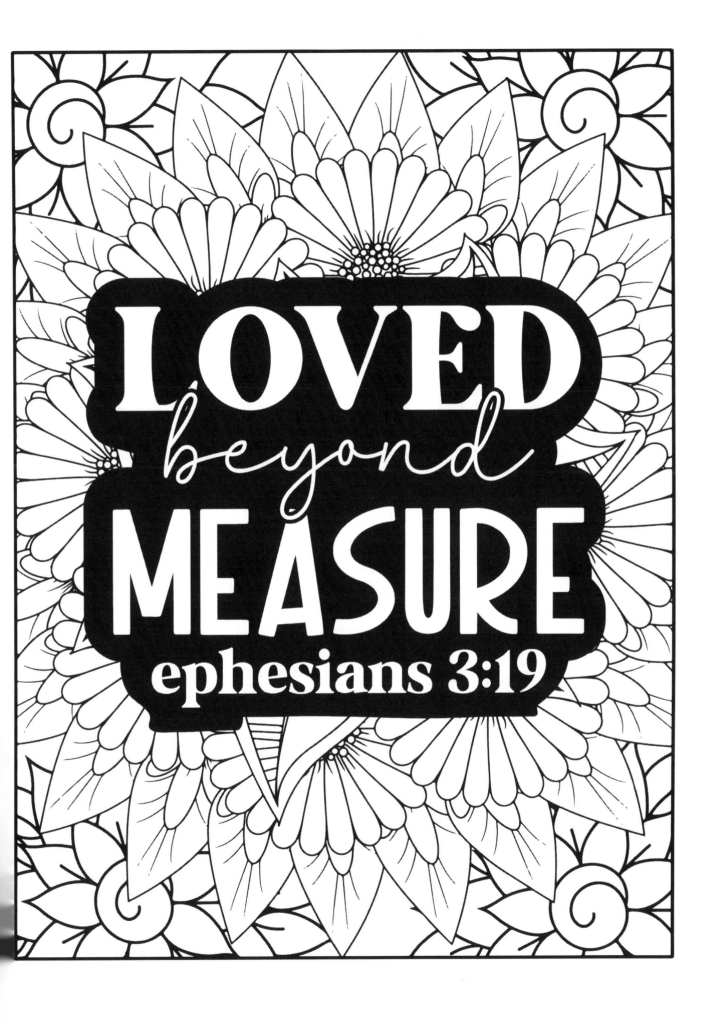

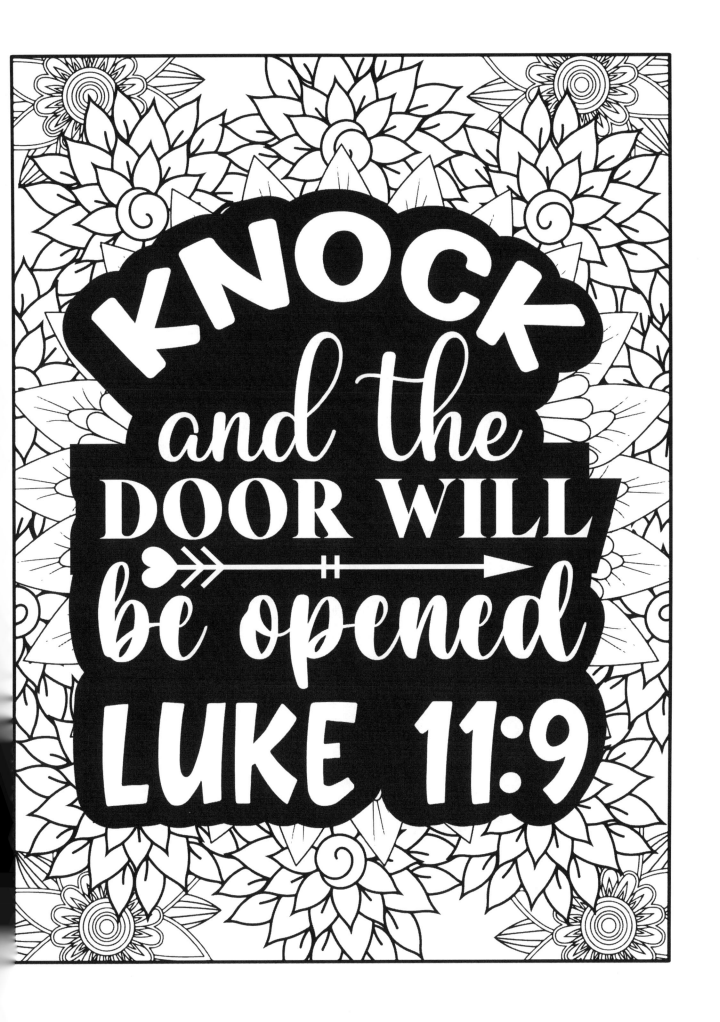

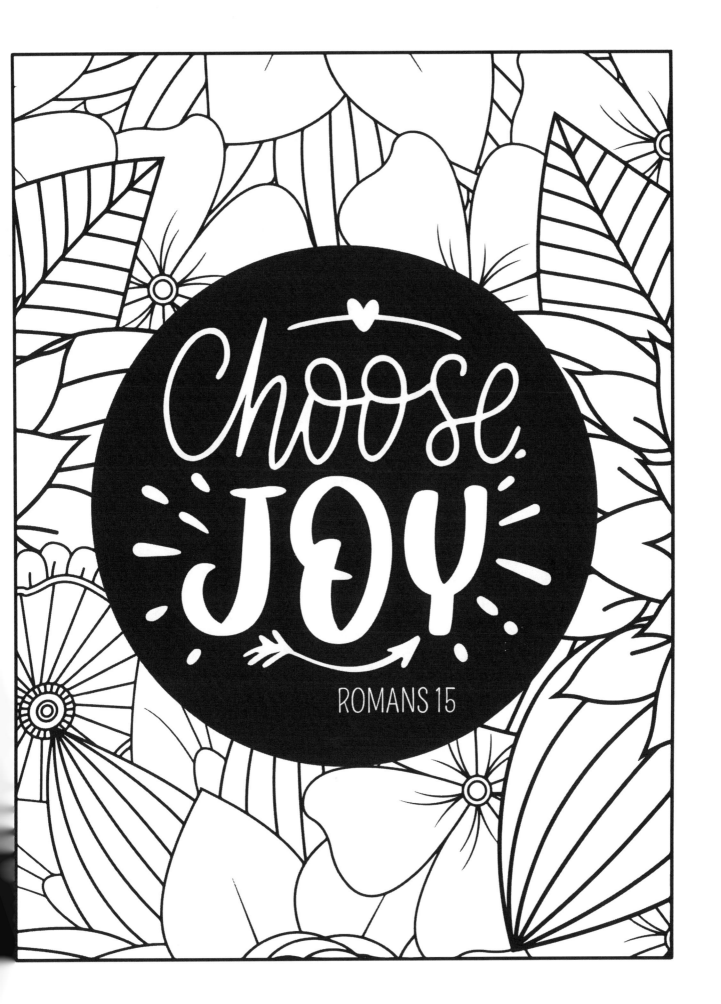

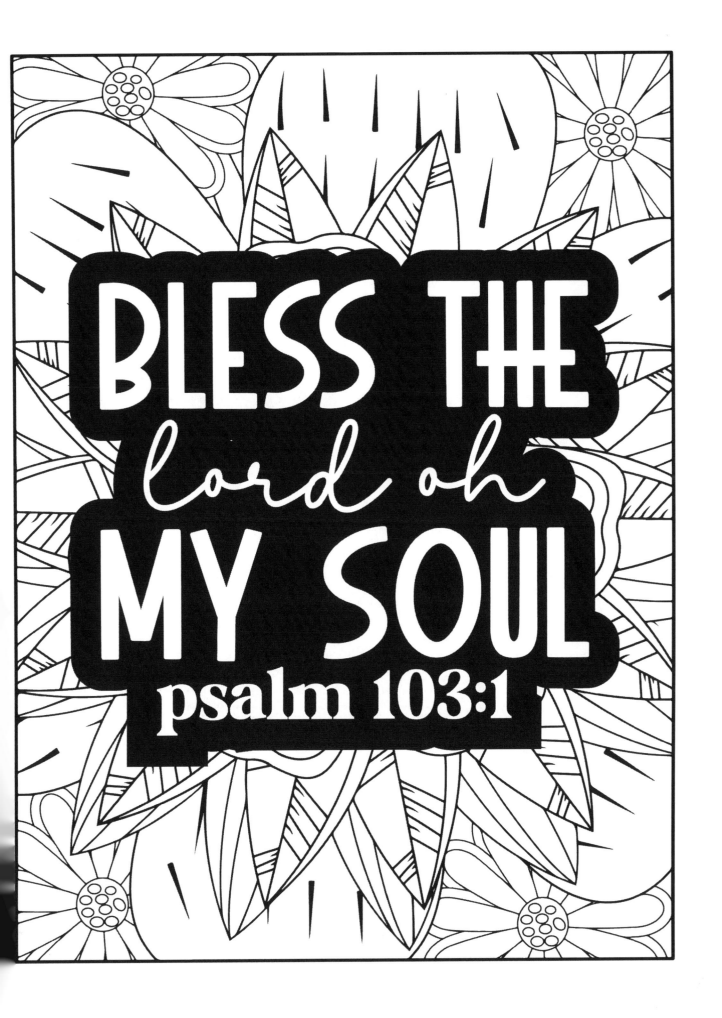

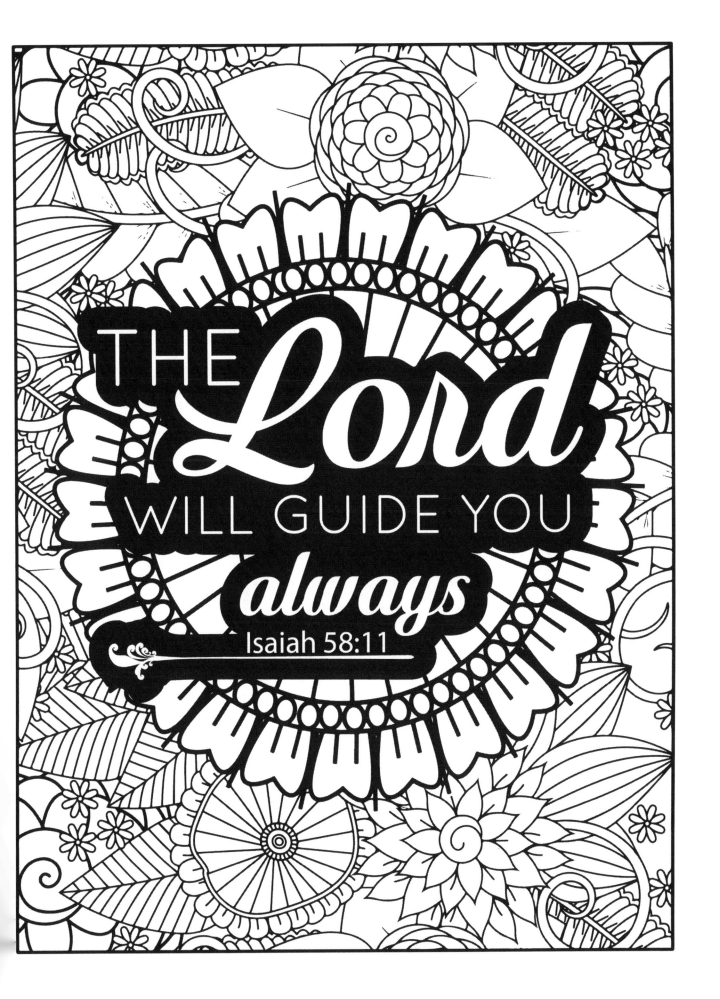

Made in United States
Orlando, FL
17 December 2024